Koalas

Willow Clark

New York

Published in 2012 by The Rosen Publishing Group, Inc.
29 East 21st Street, New York, NY 10010

First Edition

Editor: Joanne Randolph
Book Design: Julio Gil

Photo Credits: Cover, pp. 4–5, 6, 8 (left, right), 9, 10, 11, 12–13, 14 (left, right), 15, 16, 17, 18 (left, right), 19, 20–21, 22 Shutterstock.com; p. 7 © GeoAtlas RF CD.

Library of Congress Cataloging-in-Publication Data

Clark, Willow.
 Koalas / by Willow Clark. — 1st ed.
    p. cm. — (Up a tree)
 Includes index.
 ISBN 978-1-4488-6185-9 (library binding) — ISBN 978-1-4488-6329-7 (pbk.) —
 ISBN 978-1-4488-6330-3 (6-pack)
 1. Koala—Juvenile literature. I. Title.
 QL737.M384C37 2012
 599.2'5—dc23
                        2011027626

Manufactured in the United States of America

CPSIA Compliance Information: Batch #WW12PK: For Further Information contact Rosen Publishing, New York, New York at 1-800-237-9932

Contents

What's in a Name?

You may have heard a koala be called a koala bear. It might surprise you to learn that it is not a bear at all. The koala was first called a bear by English explorers in the 1700s. They thought the animal looked like a little bear. Koalas are actually a **species** of **marsupial**. Marsupials are **mammals** that have pouches.

Koalas have round heads and furry ears that stick out from the sides.

Koalas are **arboreal** animals. That means that they spend most of their time in trees. Most of their needs can be met up in trees. They even eat and sleep there. Are you ready to find out more?

The Land Down Under

Koalas live in Australia in the states of Queensland, New South Wales, and Victoria. This is where the eucalyptus trees that provide the koalas' food and shelter are the most plentiful. Koalas do not live together in groups. Instead, each adult has a home area of trees, which is close to the home areas of other koalas.

Koalas need a lot of space to live, about 100 trees for each koala.

Where Koalas Live

Timor Sea

Arafura Sea

Indian Ocean

Northern Territory

Australia

Coral Sea

Western Australia

South Australia

Queensland

New South Wales

Great Australian Bight

A.C.T

Victoria

Tasman Sea

Tasmania →

MAP KEY

Koala Range

Koalas' **habitat** can be anywhere that forests grow. The places they live generally have warm summers and cool winters. The koala's thick, woolly fur helps keep it from getting too hot or too cold. Its fur even acts like a raincoat and sheds water when it rains!

The Koala's Body

Adult koalas are between 24 and 34 inches (61–86 cm) long and weigh between 20 and 30 pounds (9–14 kg). There are a few easy ways to tell males and females apart. Males are bigger than females. Males also have patches of brown fur on

Left: Koalas have long, sharp claws that help them climb. Their fingers are positioned in a way that lets them easily grab on to tree trunks and branches. Right: Koalas from the cooler, southern part of their range are bigger than koalas from the warmer, northern part of their range.

Koalas have small eyes and do not see very well. Their noses are large, though, and they use their noses to find the best leaves to eat in the dark.

their chests. They rub these patches of fur on their home trees to mark their territories.

Koalas are well suited to life in trees. They have sharp claws to help them climb. They also have extra thick fur on their bottoms. This fur provides a nice cushion when they are sitting on tree branches.

Koala Paws

A koala's paws are **adapted** for its life in the trees. The paws are large, and each one has rough pads that help it grip branches. The koala's sharp claws come in handy for climbing.

Each of a koala's four paws has five **digits**. On the front paws two of the digits are **opposable** from the other three digits. This means these two digits can be placed against the other digits on the paw. On the koala's back paws,

Koalas' paws are strong enough to hold their weight.

there is one large, clawless opposable digit. The two middle digits are fused, or stuck, together. The koala uses this double-clawed digit to clean itself. Opposable digits give the koala a better grip on tree branches.

Koala Fun Facts

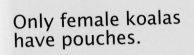

1

Only female koalas have pouches.

5

A newborn koala is about the size of a jellybean!

8

Scientists call a male koala a buck and a female koala a doe.

2

Scientists have found **fossils** of 12 species of **extinct** koalas. These koalas were much bigger than today's koalas.

3

The koala's closest relative is the wombat. Wombats are another type of marsupial that lives in Australia.

4

A koala's fur looks like it would be silky, but it really feels more like a sheep's wool.

6

Besides humans and other **primates**, koalas are one of the few animals that have fingerprints.

7

Koalas do not sweat. They cool themselves by licking their arms and stretching out on a tree branch.

9

The word "koala" comes from the Aboriginal people of Australia. These are the people who lived in Australia before European settlers.

10

Most of Earth's marsupials live in Australia or on neighboring islands. The only marsupial native to North America is the Virginia opossum.

11

Koalas do not drink much water. They get most of the water they need through their food.

Up in the Trees

What do koalas do all day up in the trees? They sleep most of the time! In fact, koalas sleep up to 18 hours each day. When they are awake, they are mostly nocturnal. This means that they are most active at night. When awake, koalas spend most of their time eating eucalyptus leaves.

Left: Koalas even sleep in the trees. They generally find forks in trees to give them safe spots to rest without falling. *Right:* Koalas come down to the ground to move between trees that are too far apart to climb over their branches.

Koalas are great at moving around in the treetops.

Koalas live alone but near other koalas. They have a good sense of hearing, which allows them to hear one another. They make noises such as grunts, bellows, screams, and snorts, as well as a noise that sounds like a long burp!

Yummy Eucalyptus!

Koalas eat eucalyptus leaves from only about 100 of the 600 different kinds of eucalyptus trees. Of those 100, each koala prefers about 6 kinds of eucalyptus leaves. The koala's sense of smell helps it tell these different kinds of leaves apart.

Koalas store food in their cheeks. There, they can keep it to eat as a snack later.

The koala has a special **digestive system** that allows it to break down these tough leaves and not be harmed by the **chemicals** in the leaves. This diet has two noticeable

Eucalyptus trees are also called gum trees. Koalas eat up to 2 pounds (1 kg) of eucalyptus leaves every day!

effects. One is that it does not give the animal a lot of energy. That is why koalas sleep so much. Another effect is that eating all that eucalyptus makes koalas smell a bit like cough drops!

Koala Predators

Koalas are most in danger of **predators** when they come to the ground to move between trees. This is because they move slowly on the ground. Koalas have few wild predators. Sometimes, though, a large

Left: Dingoes are one of koalas' main predators. They will kill koalas if they can catch them on the ground.
Right: The powerful owl, a kind of Australian owl, eats slow-moving arboreal animals, such as koalas.

People are one of the biggest dangers to koalas. They take away their habitat. Their cars also hit koalas that are crossing roads to get to new trees.

owl or a wild dog, called a dingo, will kill them.

Since people have built homes close to koala habitats, pet dogs and cats have become a threat to koalas. When dogs or cats see a koala, they often chase it and hurt or even kill the koala.

Baby Koalas

Koalas **mate** between August and February each year. The joey, or baby, is born 35 days after mating. It is only about .75 inch (2 cm) long, hairless, blind, and earless. The newborn joey stays in its mother's pouch and drinks her milk for six months while it grows.

> Koalas live for about 10 years. They are not full-grown until they are three or four years old.

At six months, the joey comes out of its mother's pouch and rides on her belly or on her back. The mother now starts to feed her young pap, a soft type of food, so that its digestive system gets stronger and it can start to eat eucalyptus leaves. When it is a year old, the young koala leaves its mother.

Koalas in Danger

Koalas were once hunted for their fur. Today, though, they are **protected** in Australia. That means it is against the law to kill, catch, or keep koalas as pets.

While koalas are protected, their habitat is not. They have lost 80 percent of their habitat due to people.

Koalas face many threats today. One of these is habitat loss. People clear eucalyptus forests to make room for housing and roads. This leaves koalas with fewer trees to call home. It puts them in danger of being killed by pets or being hit by cars. A disease that makes koalas unable to have babies is another threat koalas face. Groups such as the Australia Koala Foundation are working to help save koalas and teach people more about these magnificent marsupials.

Glossary

adapted (uh-DAPT-ed) Changed to fit new conditions.

arboreal (ahr-BOR-ee-ul) Having to do with trees.

chemicals (KEH-mih-kulz) Matter that can be mixed with other matter to cause changes.

digestive system (dy-JES-tiv SIS-tem) The body parts that help turn the food you eat into the power your body needs.

digits (DIH-jits) Fingers and toes.

extinct (ik-STINGKT) No longer existing.

fossils (FO-sulz) The hardened remains of dead animals or plants.

habitat (HA-beh-tat) The surroundings where an animal or a plant naturally lives.

mammals (MA-mulz) Warm-blooded animals that have backbones and hair, breathe air, and feed milk to their young.

marsupial (mahr-SOO-pee-ul) A type of animal that carries its young in a pouch.

mate (MAYT) To come together to make babies.

opposable (uh-POH-zuh-bel) Can be moved opposite to something else. Opposable thumbs can be moved toward and touch digits on the same hand.

predators (PREH-duh-terz) Animals that kill other animals for food.

primates (PRY-mayts) The group of animals that are more advanced than others and includes monkeys, gorillas, and humans.

protected (pruh-TEKT-ed) Kept safe.

species (SPEE-sheez) One kind of living thing. All people are one species.

Index

Web Sites

Due to the changing nature of Internet links, PowerKids Press has developed an online list of Web sites related to the subject of this book. This site is updated regularly. Please use this link to access the list:
www.powerkidslinks.com/uptr/koala/